Doctors

Laura K. Murray

CREATIVE EDUCATION • CREATIVE PAPERBACKS

seedlings

Published by Creative Education and Creative Paperbacks
P.O. Box 227, Mankato, Minnesota 56002
Creative Education and Creative Paperbacks
are imprints of The Creative Company
www.thecreativecompany.us

Design by Ellen Huber
Production by Grant Gould
Art direction by Rita Marshall
Printed in the United States of America

Photographs by Alamy (Daria Artemenko, ONOKY, Panther Media GmbH, Anatolii Riepin), iStockphoto (Michael Burrell, didesign021, Minerva Studio, monkeybusinessimages, Tinpixels), Shutterstock (fizkes, Gorodenkoff, lenetstan, Monkey Business Images, MsMaria, Sofiaworld, Tong_stocker, Valua Vitaly, wavebreakmedia, wonderisland, Elena Zajchikova)

ISBN 9781640264083 (library binding)
ISBN 9781628329414 (paperback)
ISBN 9781640005723 (eBook)

LCCN 2020907009

TABLE OF CONTENTS

Hello, doctors!

Doctors help people who are sick or hurt.

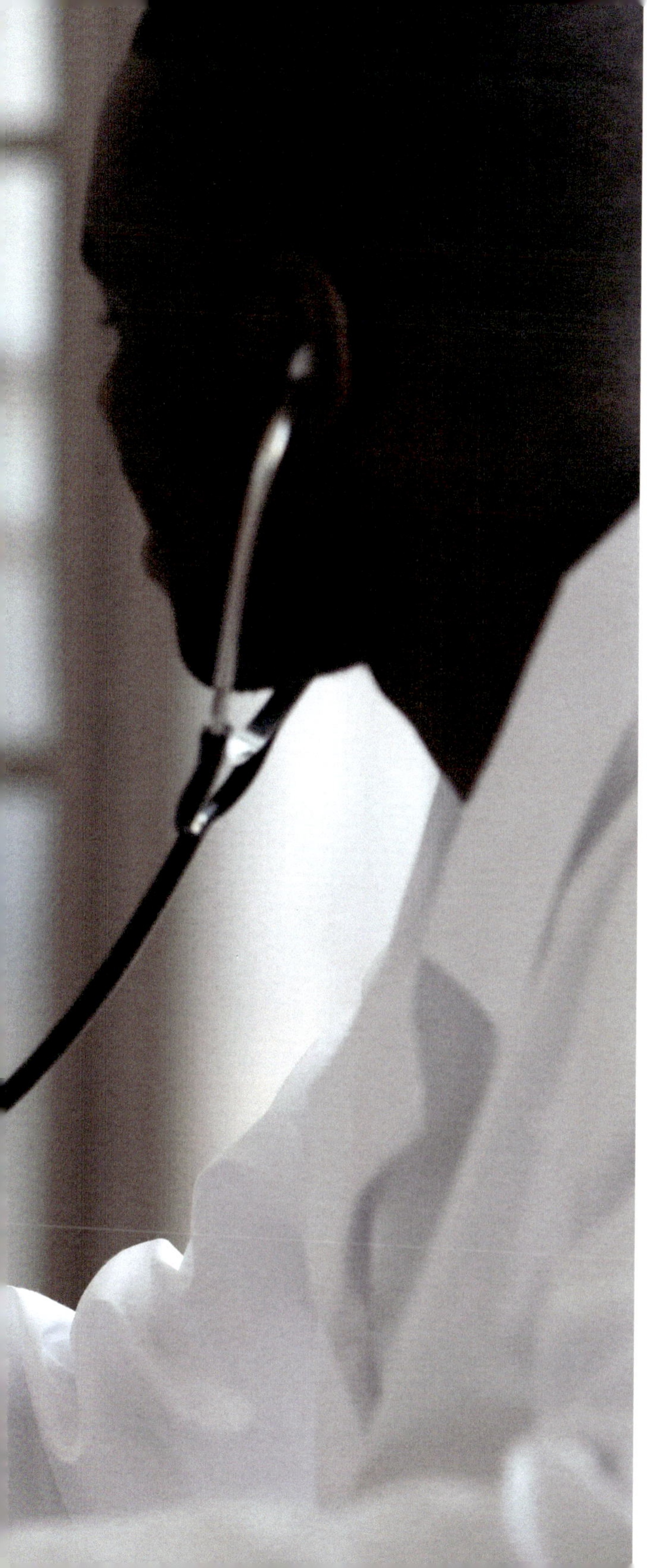

They help people stay healthy, too.

Many doctors treat **patients** in a hospital.

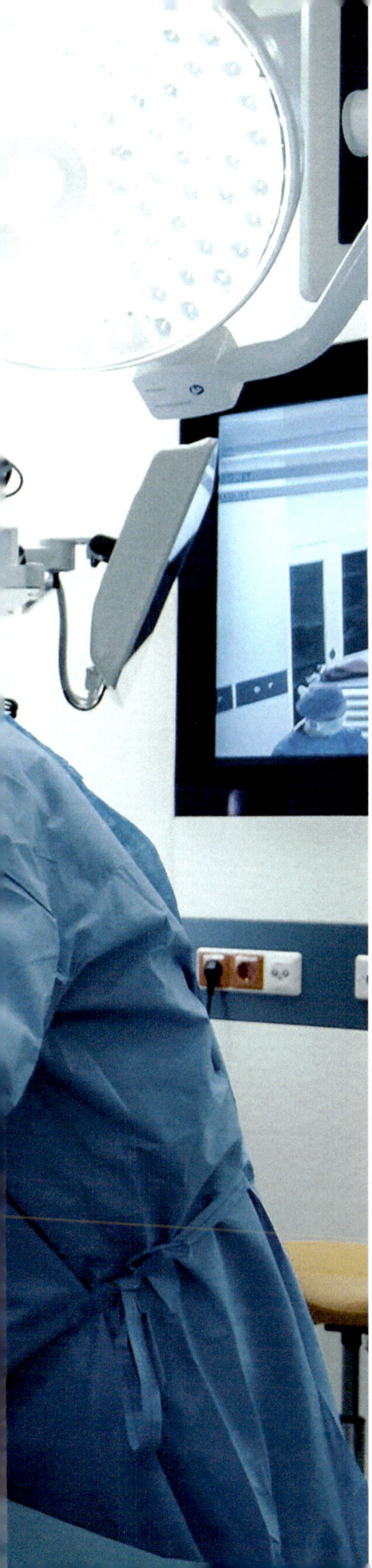

Other doctors work in an office.

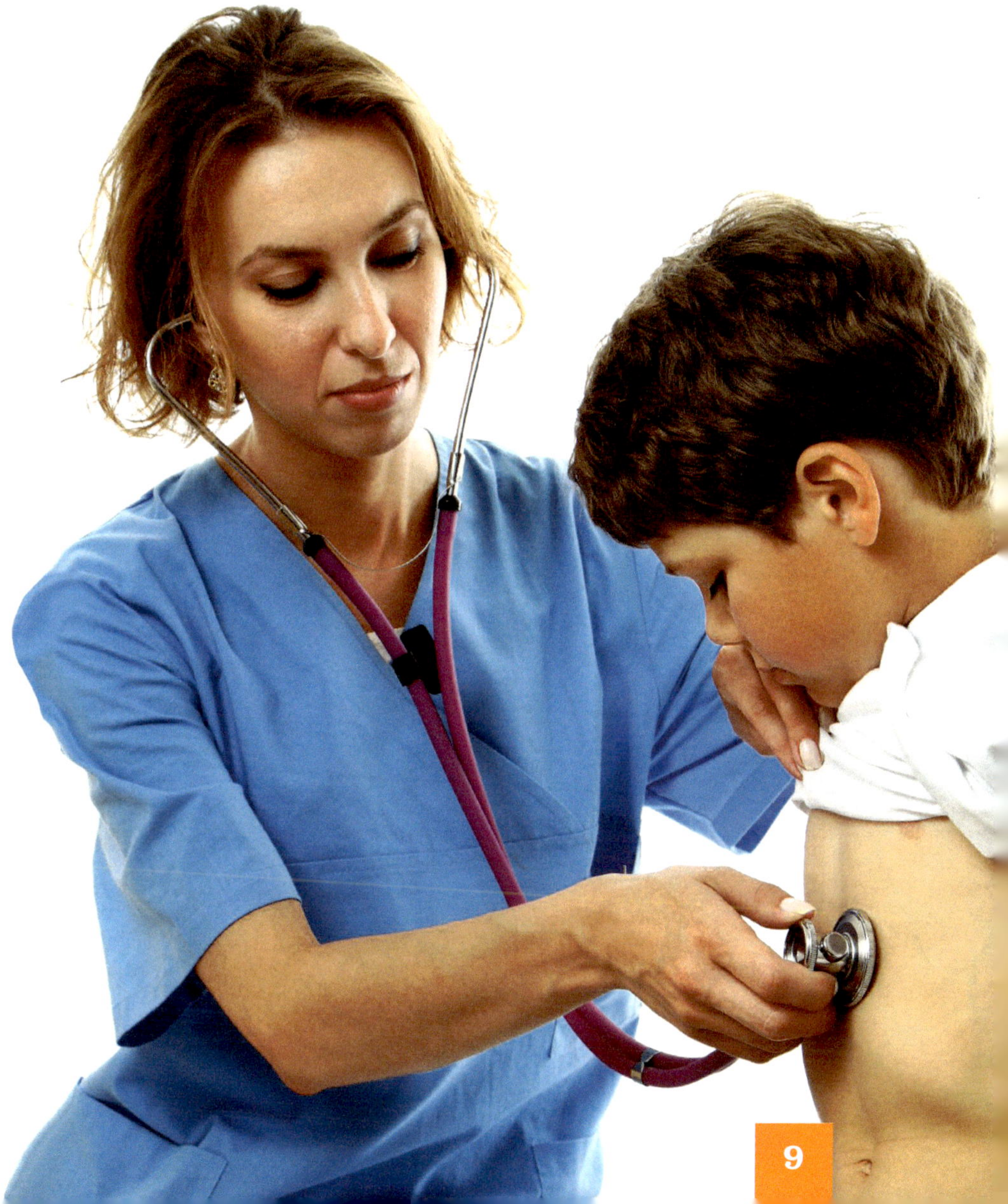

There are many kinds of doctors. Some work with children or babies.

Others treat a specific body part, such as the heart.

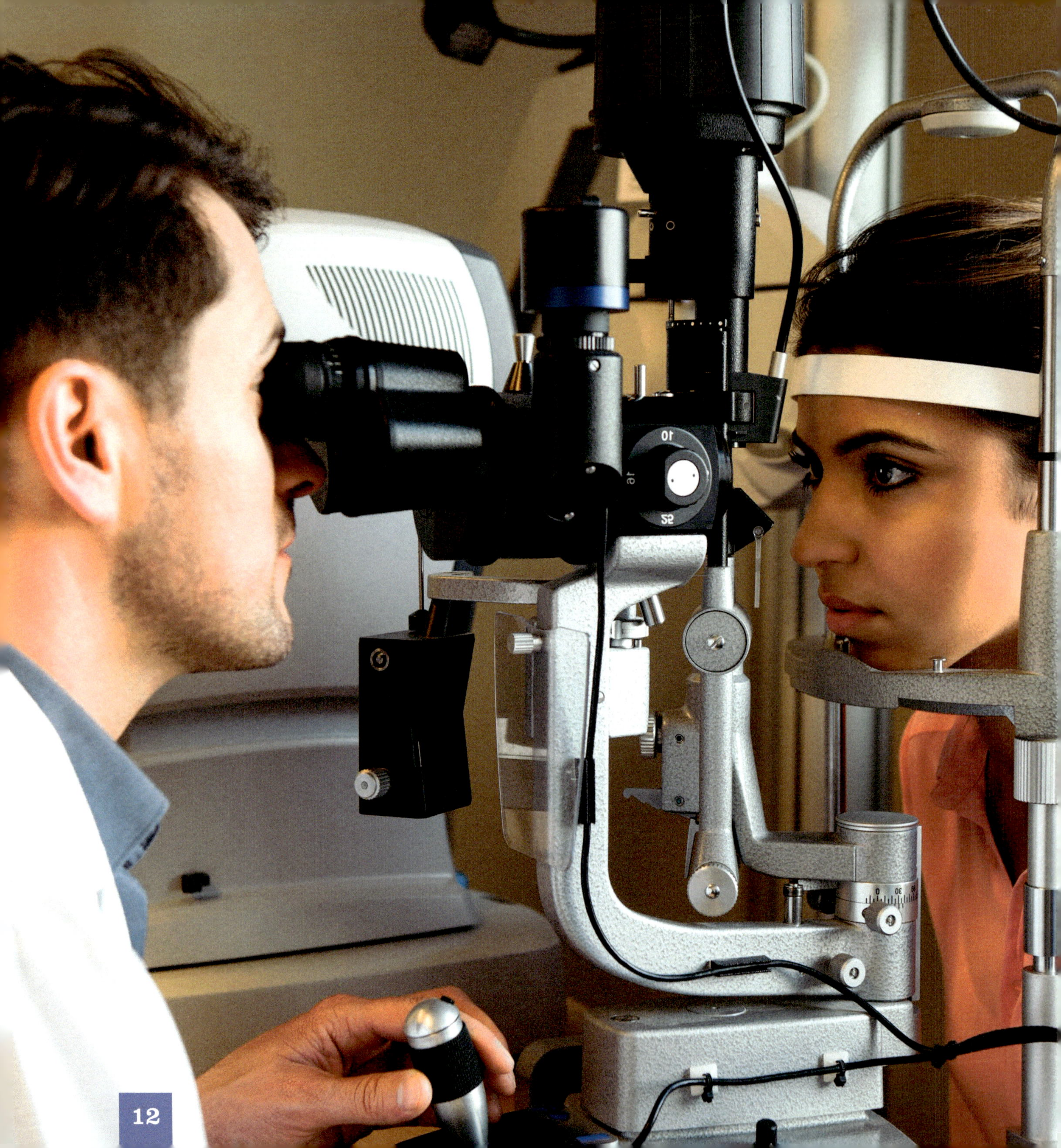

People visit doctors for checkups. Doctors make sure they are healthy.

Doctors use a **stethoscope**.

They listen to the heart and lungs. Doctors use small lights, too. They look in the eyes, ears, and throat.

Doctors try to fix what is wrong.

They give **medicine** to help people heal.

Thank you, doctors!

Picture a Doctor

light
tongue depresser
coat

Words to Know

checkups: visits to the doctor to check health

medicine: drugs used to treat illness

patients: people who are getting medical care

stethoscope: a tool used to listen to the heart, lungs, and stomach

Read More

Leaf, Christina. *Doctors*.
Minneapolis: Bellwether Media, 2018.

Rodriguez, Alicia. *Doctor's Office*.
New York: Crabtree Publishing, 2022.

Websites

Health for Kids
https://www.healthforkids.co.uk/

PBS: Doctor Daniel
https://pbskids.org/daniel/games/doctor-daniel/

Note: Every effort has been made to ensure that the websites listed above are suitable for children, that they have educational value, and that they contain no inappropriate material. However, because of the nature of the Internet, it is impossible to guarantee that these sites will remain active indefinitely or that their contents will not be altered.

Index